BUTCHER BAKER COCKTAIL MAKER

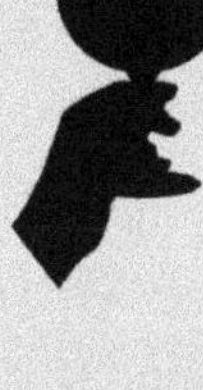

BUTCHER BAKER COCKTAIL MAKER

A Guide to
Making and Shaking

Written and Illustrated by

Natalie E. Brown

First Published in the United States of America in 2021 by Natalie E. Brown

ISBN: 978-0-578-91840-2
Library of congress control number: 2021910798

First edition

Set in Cormorant Garamond and Cheque

natalieebrown.com

*All recipes in this book are for one drink, unless otherwise specified

This book is for my family,
for whom I originally began putting together these recipes.

For my Parents who let me use them as taste testers, no matter how gross the combinations were at times.

And for my Grandparents, who were the first to open my eyes to the rich and culture filled world of wining and dining.

xo

Natalie

♥

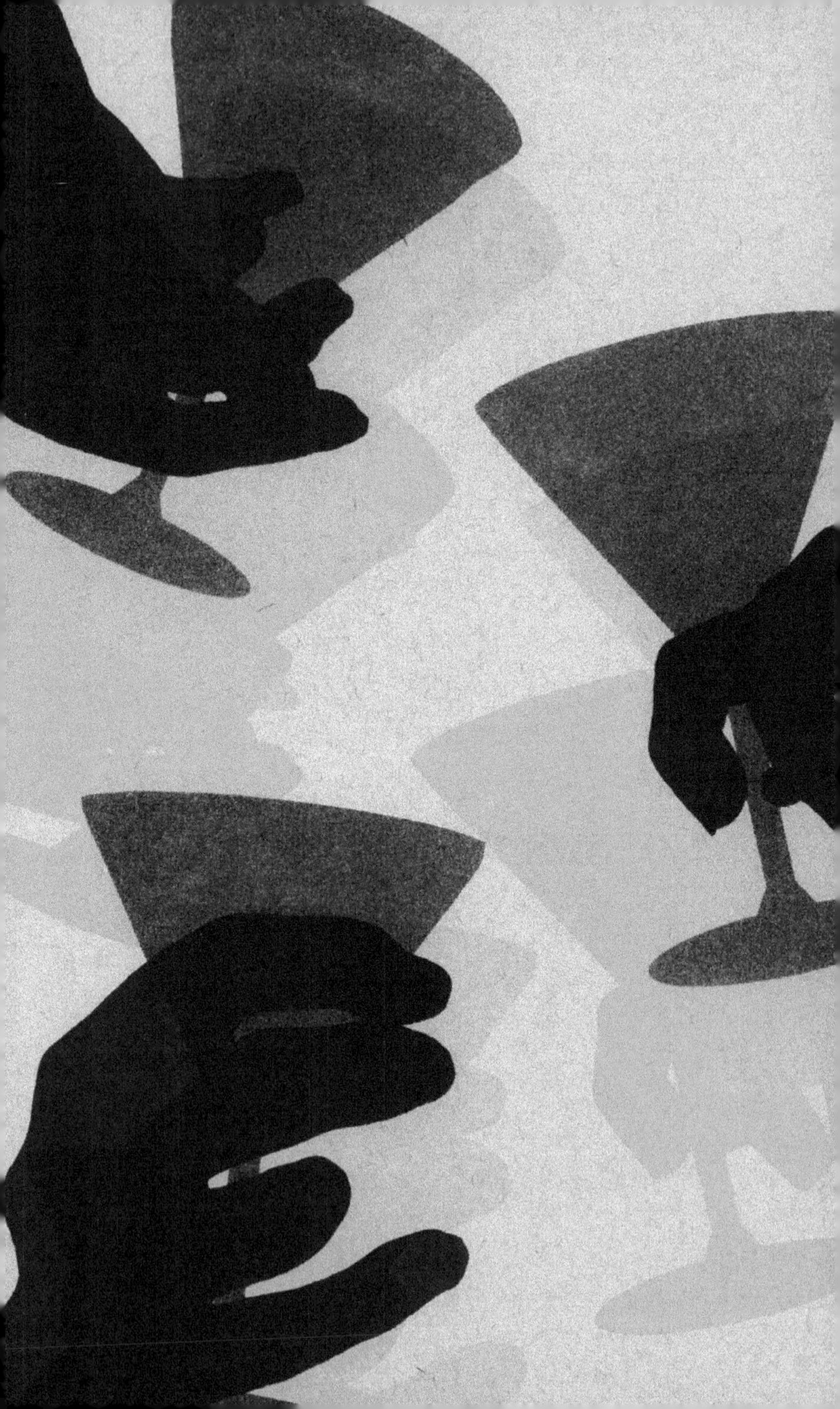

TABLE OF CONTENTS

AUTHOR'S NOTE

My life has been intertwined with cocktails and good spirits long before I became of drinking age. When I was little, I would toddle about family gatherings observing everyone laughing and having a good time - getting sips and refilling beverages for a cheeky dollar bill tip if I could wheedle it out of them. It didn't take long after that for me to become interested in what was actually in the drinks I was handling, and when I became older I became more and more mesmerized by the variety and tastes that could be achieved, especially when ingredients were combined. It was because of those experiences, with my good fortune in being able to travel and taste the world, that I have always associated cocktails with merriment, history, and culture - undoubtedly renewing my interest into adulthood.

Like the English nursery rhyme involving the butcher, the baker, and the candlestick maker, though here 'cocktail maker', this book is named for the multifaceted and rich nature with which the topic of drink making can be, and for the busybody who wrote it. Not unknown to do a large and wide variety of things in my professional practice, I have been known to seem as though I embody the work of three in one body. I feel that the composition of cocktails is no different, at times calling upon one's skills as a sommelier just as often as that of a chef, an artist, and so on...

AUTHOR'S NOTE

I wrote this collection of recipes, and short histories, to embody those feelings that I learned early on: to celebrate when and what you mix, no matter how random or small the occasion, and to learn something along the way. I hope you enjoy it!

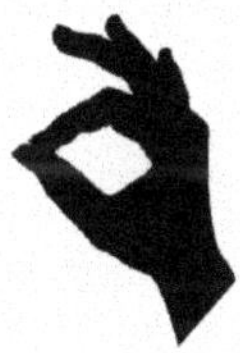

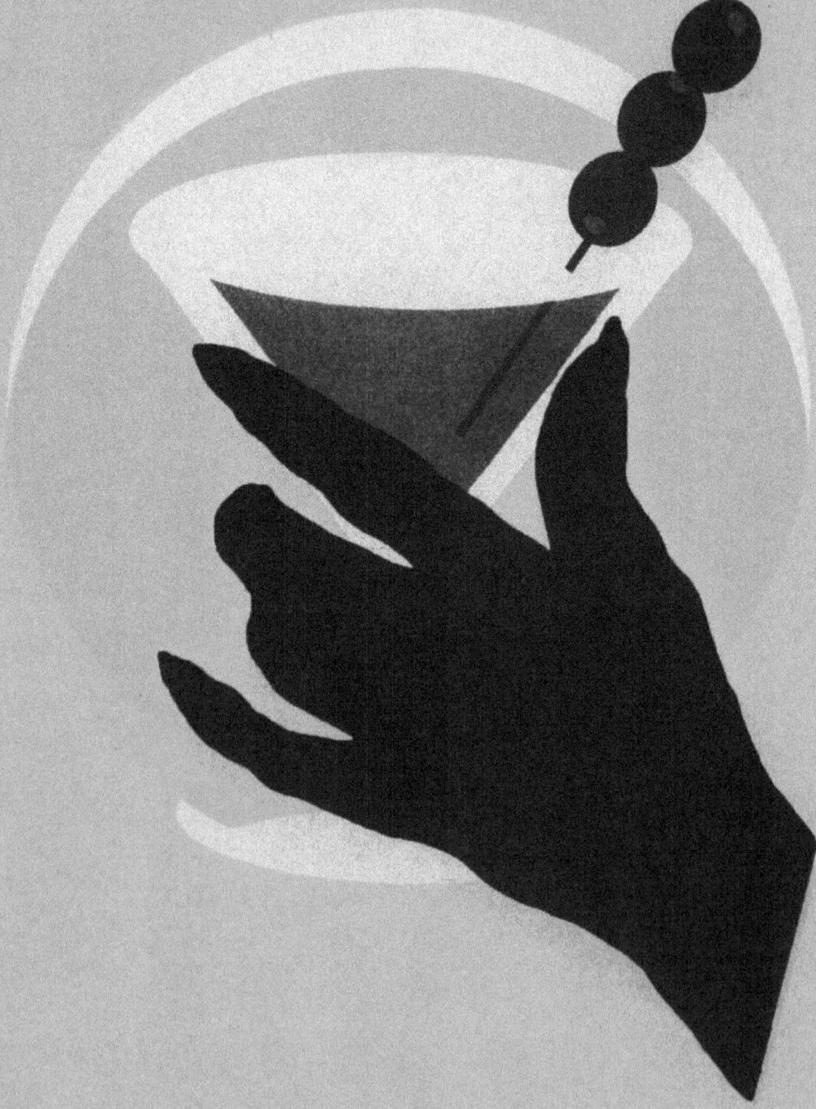

II.

MOLECULAR GASTRONOMY

Molecular Gastronomy *noun*
preparing and cooking food according to the scientific principles of what changes happen to different foods when they are cooked or combined with other foods.

Whether or not we notice through the distracting deliciousness of a freshly made cocktail, each successful one is built out of layers; I identify these as the base, body, and aroma - all of which work together to make that drink you have in your hand. The crafting of the perfect drink can be as complex or simple as you like, but for me, starting simply, and adding complexity on a case by case basis is the key to success. Thus our three groups:

Base: The base refers to the alcohol or alcohols used: the simplest yet arguably most important choice(s). Know your goal of how you want your drink to hit your palette, then you can make an informed decision on what your best choice is. Will you err on the side of sweet or sour, bitter or herbal, or a complex combination? Use that information to help you make a drink that will excite and entice your taste buds, and avoid the calamity of flatness, or an overwhelm of any one flavor. Unless of course that's your goal, that's your business.

MOLECULAR GASTRONOMY

Body: The second is body, the main volume flavor profile other than our base, and can be anything A to Z. Think pineapple to your rum, or vermouth to bourbon. This area especially appeals to the four basic taste profiles the tongue senses: sweet, salty, sour, and bitter, and will of course be different depending on the alcohol you add into. On a simpler level, I think of this as a juice or flavor additive that is immediately noticeable, but again, can be complicated by herbs, spices, and other essences, making your mix as mysterious as desired.

Aroma: Aroma in this case, not only refers to the smell of the drink but its delicate flavors or "top notes". The easiest way to think of this for me is as a flavor or scent detail, such as a faint floral note at the end of a wine.

Smell makes up approximately 80% of taste, and will be the first enticement to a cocktail; a make or break moment. So, think about your smells, the smell of the alcohol, the smell of the body mix, the garnishes, and how they all work together to create a cohesive and delicious effect. This sounds complicated, and it can be, but trust your nose, it's the first sign of a delicious drink coming your way.

MOLECULAR GASTRONOMY

Extras: I don't technically categorize this as part of my big three because it varies so drastically for each individual drink, and some drinks are perfect without a thing. They are, however, still an important consideration. When mixing a drink these extras are, largely, a part of the finishing touch, but they are often the significant first impression your beverage will make to you or your guest. Extras include garnishes, like mint and citrus, ground spices added atop, or a shaken egg white thrown in for a velvety textured froth. Don't be afraid of the egg white; I was skeptical at first too!

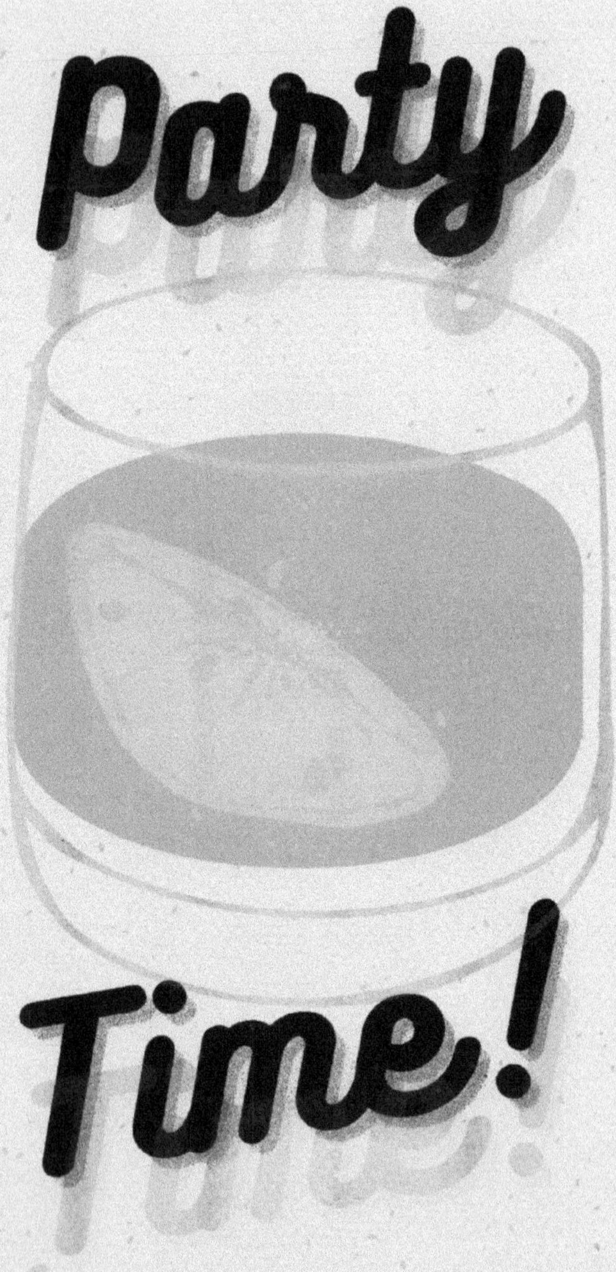
Party
Time!

15.

STOCKING YOUR BAR

Equipment: liquors, glasses, fruit, and more: it seems like a lot, and everyone seems to have a different opinion on what the "right" combination is. But this is highly personal, truly. Everyone might say you need "this" aperitif, or you just *have* to keep a bottle of that wine, but it doesn't make any sense to stock something if you loathe it, right? You're never going to touch those recipes anyway! The following is a list of basic equipment for a well-rounded bar set, adjust as you see fit, and most importantly, love everything you add! Not everything needs to be in your stock all of the time if you haven't got the space or a bar cart. Just make sure you've got everything you need for your repertoire of drink making, and any special occasions you've got coming up. The most important thing to remember when stocking your bar is quality. You don't need to always get top shelf or the rarest of ingredients, but making sure that your fruits, and juices are fresh and freshly squeezed and your alcohols are of an ironclad caliber is the difference between a mediocre and marvelous beverage.

Not sure if you love something, or are nervous to try it? Go to your closest friend or family member who has it and pilfer a sample off of them. It is an odd ask, but always a fun get together to try new things with your favorite people.

STOCKING YOUR BAR

Liquors:
- gin
- vodka
- tequila
- rum (light)
- rum (dark)
- white rum
- rye whiskey
- blended scotch
- absinthe, or chartreuse
- bourbon

Liquid Extras:
- simple syrup (pp.90)
- sweet and dry vermouth
- Angostura bitters
- grenadine
- champagne and/or other sparkling wine
- Sweet wines: Such as Lillet Blanc, and a red Moscato.
-heavy cream, and/or half and half

Juices:
- lemon
- lime
- orange
- cranberry
- pineapple
- tomato

(and your other favorites, including any nectars)
- club soda
- tonic water
- lemon-lime soda
- ginger ale and/or ginger beer

Liqueurs:
- orange liqueur
- chocolate liqueur
- mint liqueur
- schnapps of your choice flavorings
- Kahlúa
- créme de cassis
- Drambuie
- Campari
- Aperol
- Pimm's No. 1

STOCKING YOUR BAR

Equipment:

- measurement tools: cups and spoons (I find ounces and teaspoons the most helpful to deal with in small batches).
- cocktail shaker and strainer
- jiggers
- citrus squeezer
- muddler
- bottle opener, and corkscrew
- grater
- peeler
- a blender, or the vivacity to replace it

Garnishes and other Extras:

- lemons
- limes
- oranges
- maraschino cherries
- spices: preferably ground (nutmeg, cinnamon)
- herbs: (mint, basil, cilantro)
- green olives
- sugar (finely granulated and cubed)
- cream of coconut, and/or coconut milk

GLASSWARE

There are thousands of glasses for thousands of drinks. These are the simply the basics.

Collins - Often interchangeable with the highball glass, the collins glass is slightly slimmer and holds 10-14 ounces. This glass is great for fizz as the narrowness keeps the bubbles from dissipating too quickly.

Coupe - The traditional champagne glass has a slew of legends surrounding it, perhaps most notably that it was modelled after Marie Antoinette's left breast, and presented to her as a gift. There is, however, mention of the first early coupe glass in England a century before Antoinette. I fancy the former myself. A squat bowl shape, it measures 5-7 ounces.

Flute or tulip - A glass with a tall, long shape to keep the bubbles bubbling and help preserve and present the aromatic elements. It's usually a 6-ounce glass with a 4-ounce pour of drink.

Highball - Often interchangeable with the collins glass, the highball glass is a tall straight-sided glass with many uses. Usually 9- 10-ounce or 12- 14-ounce size.

GLASSWARE

Hurricane - This large, usually 20-ounce glass was invented to resemble the oil hurricane lamps that were used until the 19th century. It has a circular base and curves up into an outturned trumpet shape.

Irish Coffee - The Irish Coffee glass was designed for a multitude of hot beverages, with heat resistant glass, sometimes metal, and a handle to keep your hands nice and cool. It holds 8-10 ounces.

Margarita - This glass is unique as it was designed specifically for the drink it is named for. The most typical sizes are 6-8 ounces and 10-14 ounces, and people usually size up depending on whether their drinks will have ice or not. It is also used for a slew of blended beverages with an icy or slushy texture.

Martini - A classic, triangular silhouetted glass with a stem, suited for a plethora of drinks. They are made in as little as 3 ounces and as many as 12 ounces.

GLASSWARE

Old Fashioned - A short, bottom-heavy glass with straight edges, sometimes called a whiskey glass. It typically has a 4- to 10-ounce capacity. The Double Old Fashioned glass is the same concept, but larger, at 12-16 ounces. Both are used for drinks on the rocks, and their heavy bottoms are able to stand in-glass muddling.

Pint - Used almost exclusively for beer, either bottled or tap, the 16-ounce pint glass is best when placed in the freezer, allowing frosting to occur for a thoroughly cooled through beverage.

Port Wine - Also used for sherry and liqueurs, this little 1- 3 ounce glass has a little stem and a squatty flute-like shape. It resembles a small hurricane glass.

Red Wine - This is the traditional wine glass shape we would all recognize in a lineup. It's larger than that of the white wine glass with the purpose of allowing better aromatic exposure. It is, however, smaller than the balloon wine glass, which is rounder and larger. It is also used for fizzy beverages, and holds 12-14 ounces.

GLASSWARE

White Wine - With a smaller and more narrow shape than the red wine glass, this glass holds 8-12 ounces. It keeps everything close together with the aim of keeping the wine chilled.

Shot - The shot glass is a thick, stout, little thing resembling a mini Old Fashioned glass, and measuring 1 ½ ounces, though it comes in larger sizes. The shot glass is used both as a measurement tool and as a vessel for shots of liquor such as tequila, vodka, or rum. Cordial glasses hold the same amount of liquid, but are trumpet shaped with a short stem.

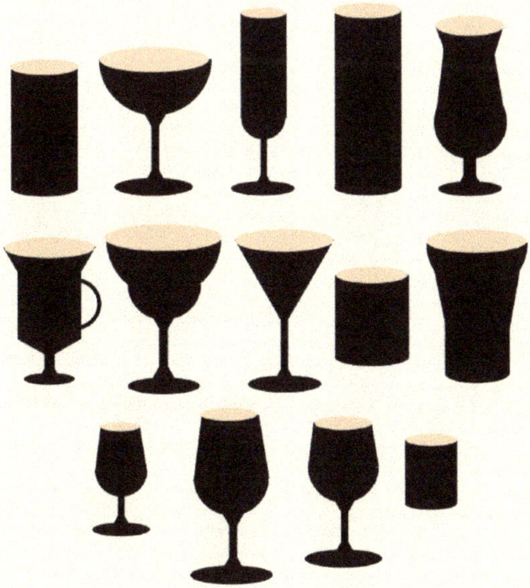

ALCOHOLS

The following are the types of alcohol that are used in the recipes of this book.

Absinthe - Absinthe is a spirit made from a variety of herbs, perhaps most notably aniseed and fennel. Famed among writers of the 19th and 20th centuries, it has a long mythological history of being a hallucinogen, though modern research does not support these claims. This idea is most likely rooted in absinthe's extremely high alcohol content of about 90% ABV (alcohol by volume), and the chemical thujone, present in wormwood. The original recipe was first produced in 1797, by Henry-Louis Pernod (1776 -1851) who later established a factory in Pontellier, France. However, after being made illegal in Switzerland and later France after the turn of the 20th century, the Pernod Fils company was established in Spain in 1918 to fulfill the demand across Europe.

Gin - Gin is a clear, distilled spirit made from juniper berries and often has other botanicals mixed in. While it comes in multiple varieties such as pink gin and sloe gin (from sloe berries), traditional distilled gin has anywhere from 30 to 50% ABV.

ALCOHOLS

The name comes from the French genièvre meaning juniper berry. It was later changed to the Dutch genever, likely by the man who began to distill it—Franciscus Sylvius, a professor of medicine at the University of Leiden of Holland (1614 –1672). Sylvius distilled the juniper berry brew as an alternative to more expensive medicines with diuretic properties, as the juniper berry was popular during the 17th century. Of course, the name later changed to the English gin as we know and love it today, becoming a popular liquor in everyone's cabinet.

Rum - This traditionally Caribbean beverage is made from sugarcane, sometimes molasses, and includes a range of light to dark varieties from different islands, all fermented. Typically, rum has a concentration of around 40% ABV, but some overproof reaches over 75%. The first records of rum come from Barbados in 1650, where it was already being traded throughout the West Indies. Its first name, however, was not rum, as it was referred to as "kill-devil" later "rumbullion." It wasn't until after the 1670s that it changed to just "rum" as we all know it today.

ALCOHOLS

Tequila - Tequila is a type of liquor that dwells under the umbrella of mezcal, which includes many liquors made from any of the agave plant and its variations. The main ingredient of tequila however, is the blue agave plant, traditionally grown in Mexico. The cooked plant's fructose is used to distill the beverage, and the ABV is usually about 40%. The name comes from the Mexican town Tequila in the state of Jalisco where it originated, and is still produced today.

Vodka - Vodka, originally distilled from fermented potatoes and now other grains, is a very versatile alcohol. It has an ABV of 40% in the United States, however, its proof varies based on the country of origin and their individual regulations. Some of the strongest ABV vodka in the world is as high as 96%. "Vodka" comes from the Russian word вода (Voda), meaning water, due to its colorlessness and odorlessness. Its origins are murky to say the least, but it is generally agreed to have originated in either Poland or Russia, and is documented in the 14th century despite claims of its birth as early as the 8th.

Whiskey - First found in ancient Mesopotamia, then the UK, and now in North America, whiskey is a spirit made from fermented grain (corn, rye, barley or wheat). The ABV is anywhere from 40% to 50%.

ALCOHOLS

Currently, the United States of America is the largest producer and consumer of whiskey, though the first reference to its usage on paper is from Scotland in 1494. Each country and indeed producer of the drink uses different variables that give their brew a distinct flavor and reputation. These variables can include, but are not limited to: grain used, aging time, aging conditions, and wood barrel type. The spelling 'whiskey' is Irish and American, and 'whisky' is used by the Scottish and Japanese.

Wine - Made, of course, from sun-ripened grapes going through fermentation processes, wine is one of the most popular alcoholic beverages today, and comes in multiple variations beyond red and white. Champagne, and it's Italian cousin prosecco, as well as sweet and dry vermouths, which are fortified, are all wines. Most wine has less than 15% ABV. Other fortified and sparkling wines contain between 12 and 20% ABV. Wine is quite possibly the oldest alcoholic beverage, with the *Vitis Vinifera*, the grape type almost exclusively used for wine making, being cultivated in the Middle East as early as 4000 BCE. That same grape genus later travelled through human intervention to Greece, then Italy and the Alsatian region of France, and eventually traveled all through Europe establishing vineyards and wineries which are often still found in the same places today touting wine's popularity.

CLASSICS

28.

COSMOPOLITAN

2 oz. vodka
1 ½ oz. cranberry juice (no sugar added)
¾ oz. lime juice
¾ oz. orange liqueur
Orange twist for garnish

Add all ingredients to a cocktail shaker, add ice, and shake vigorously for at least 20 seconds. Strain into martini or cosmo glass. Garnish with an orange twist.

29.

DARK AND STORMY

1 ½ oz. spiced rum (dark)
Juice of 1/2 lime, and an additional 1/2 lime wedge for garnish
4 oz. ginger beer, chilled

In a mixing glass with ice, add your rum, lime juice, and ginger beer and stir slowly around the edge until chilled through. Strain into an Old Fashioned glass (with fresh ice, if desired) and garnish with lime.

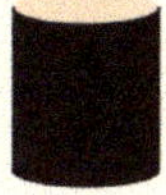

30.

GIMLET

Since the late 18th century, when the Royal Navy started to treat scurvy with citrus, the combination of lime to gin was popularized with a drink similar to the gin and tonic. An early gimlet however, might have looked a lot more like a grog, sometimes with quinine or even rum!

2 ½ oz. gin
¾ oz. lime juice
½ oz. simple syrup (pp.90)
Lime wheel to garnish

Add all liquid ingredients to a cocktail shaker, add ice, and shake until chilled. Strain into an Old Fashioned glass, and garnish with a lime wheel.

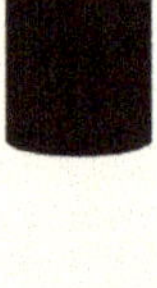

31.

GIN AND TONIC

The gin and tonic was first created at the end of the 19th century, when British soldiers in India started adding some of their gin rations to their medicinal quinine tonic to cut the bitterness. Sometimes sugar would be added for sweetness, if sweetened gin (then called, tom gin) wasn't already being used, and lime was readily at hand in the hot eastern climate. The combination just made sense, and it has been a British staple ever since.

2 oz. gin
5 oz. tonic water
Juice of ½ lime
Lime wheel for garnish.

Add all ingredients slowly to a highball glass over ice, stir well, and garnish with lime.

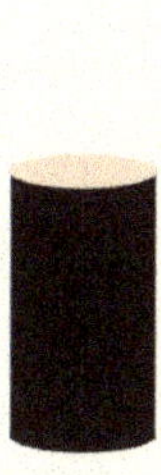

GIN FIZZ

*This is the G&T's sweeter, more elegant cousin.

2 oz. gin
1 oz. lemon juice
¾ oz. simple syrup (pp.90)
1 egg white
1 oz. club soda

*Discretion is advised when consuming any and all raw ingredients.

Add gin, lemon juice, simple syrup, and the egg white to a cocktail shaker and do a dry shake (when you shake a cocktail without adding ice to the shaker) until the egg white is foamy. Then, add ice to the shaker and repeat with a wet shake to chill through the mixture. Strain into a highball glass over fresh ice cubes, and add club soda. Stir to incorporate completely before serving.

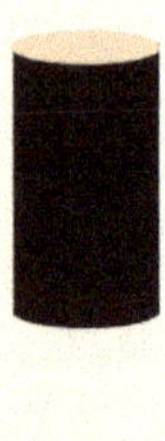

33.

MANHATTAN

I didn't particularly understand until I moved to Europe that the concept of the maraschino cherry is a little different on opposite sides of the Atlantic. In America, they are brightly colored, preserved in a thin sugar liquid, and while the concept is the same on the continent, they are dark, in a thick sugary liquid and hold their firmness much better. Both are delicious, but check out the latter if you are skewering or floating them in your drink as they allow less liquid to permeate them and make them soggy! I like to use the brand Luxardo which are traditional Italian maraschinos, which you can order online quite easily.

2 oz. rye whiskey (or bourbon)
1 ¼ oz. sweet red vermouth
3 dashes Angostura bitters
1 small spoonful maraschino syrup from the cocktail cherries (about ¼ oz.)
A maraschino cherry to garnish

Add all ingredients to a cocktail shaker with plenty of ice, and shake well until chilled. Strain into a martini glass and garnish with a maraschino cherry or two, and serve straight.

MARGARITA

Starting my cocktail journey with margarita mixes, I thought they were fine but nothing too special. Oh my gosh was I wrong, and the only difference is making them yourself and with freshly squeezed limes! It's a game changing switch everyone should make immediately.

Lime to rim and garnish
Salt or sugar for coating rim
1 oz. Cointreau
1 1/2 oz. lime juice
2 oz. tequila
½ oz. simple syrup (pp.90)

Rub the rim of a margarita glass with a lime, then dip the moistened rim in either salt or sugar, depending on your taste (salt is traditional). In a cocktail shaker, mix all liquid ingredients with ice until well chilled, and strain into the glass carefully so as not to shift any of the rimming. Additionally garnish with a lime wedge or round.

MARTINI

Shaken or stirred?

Traditionally, drinks composed solely of spirits are stirred, especially ones with gin so as not to "bruise" the botanicals. This concern is minimized considerably if you are making your martinis with vodka, and helps to chill the liquid more thoroughly if you prefer. This is why chilling the glass for a stirred version helps to keep its temperature down without sacrificing the drink's quality - sorry James Bond!

½ oz. dry vermouth
3 oz. gin (or vodka)
Garnish with a green olive or lemon twist

*A splash of olive juice added to the mixing glass makes it "dirty", if desired.
*A garnish of a pearl onion instead of olives creates what is called a Gibson.

Add all ingredients to a mixing glass with ice and stir well. Strain into a chilled martini glass neat, garnish, and enjoy!

I'll Drink To That

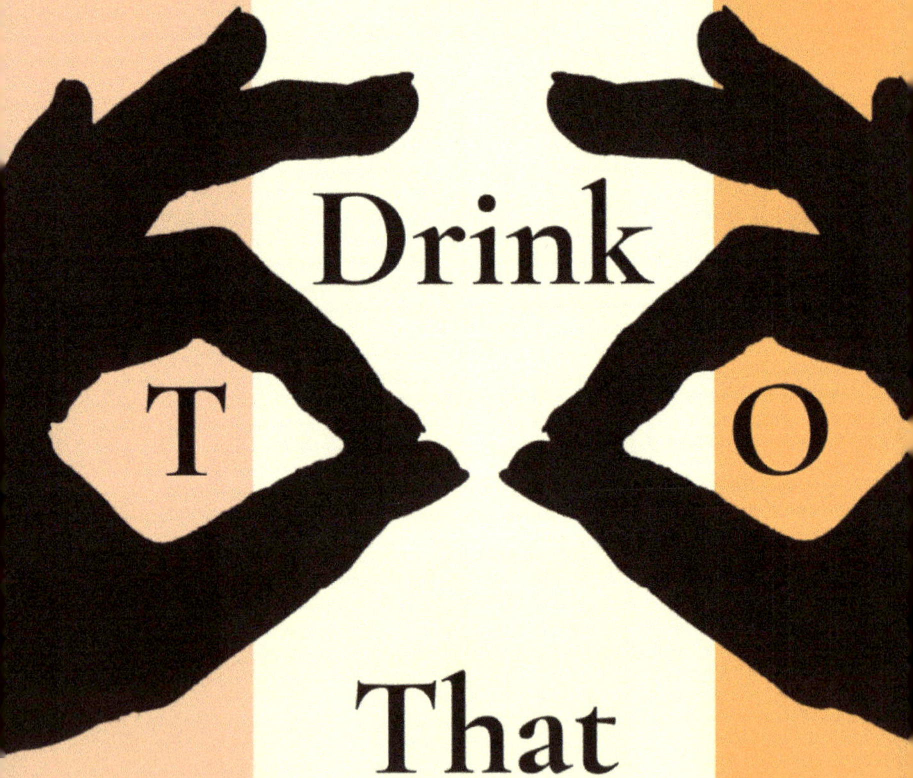

MIMOSA

These aren't just for bridal showers and ladies luncheons everyone! Mimosa's make a great celebratory drink for any occasion, or are a great way to use up spare champagne and/or prosecco in a recipe containing another ingredient we all have - OJ!

3 oz. orange juice
4 oz. champagne or prosecco

Add orange juice to a champagne flute, and top with champagne. Stir gently, and serve.

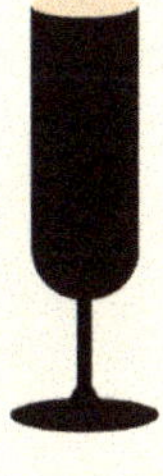

MINT JULEP

A small handful of mint leaves, save some for garnish
1 sugar cube
¼ oz. lime juice
¼ oz. simple syrup (pp.90)
2 oz. bourbon
4 oz. club soda

In a mixing glass, add the mint, sugar cube, lime juice, and simple syrup and thoroughly muddle them together, allowing the mint to infuse into the liquid. Add the mixture to a highball glass with ice, and add bourbon and club soda. Stir well, and garnish with a sprig of mint.

*It's typical to add the muddled mint to the final drink to allow the full essence to be transferred, along with continual infusion. If you prefer a cleaner look, you can remove the muddled mint leaves when you add the sugar mixture to the glass.

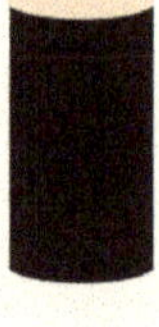

39.

NEGRONI

This Northern Italian-born beverage is a derivative of the Americano cocktail, already made throughout Italy and named for its popularity among the American tourists in the beginning of the 20th century. The Negroni, however, was supposedly created when a Count Camillo Negroni requested the soda water in the Americano drink be replaced with gin. This version caught on quickly with the masses.

1 oz. gin
1 oz. Campari
1 oz. sweet vermouth (red)
¼ oz. simple syrup (pp.90)
Orange twist to garnish

In a mixing glass, add all liquid ingredients over ice and stir for at least 30 seconds. Strain into an Old Fashioned glass, and garnish with an orange twist.

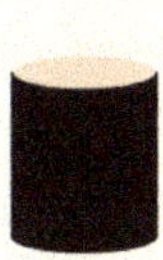

OLD FASHIONED

This thoroughly American "old fashioned whiskey cocktail" as it was originally called, can be traced back to the Pendennis Club in Louisville Kentucky from the late nineteenth century. Though likely invented in various forms long before then all across America, it was here that the drink was revived and made so popular using none other than the classic Kentucky bourbon whiskey made from rye mash. American rye whiskey must be comprised of at least 51% rye mash, setting it apart from others which are based mainly with corn.

1 sugar cube
3 dashes Angostura bitters
A few dashes of water
2 oz. rye whiskey
Garnish with a maraschino cherry

Add the sugar cube to an Old Fashioned glass, and saturate with bitters and dashes of water. Muddle until dissolved, then cover with rye whiskey. Stir well until completely incorporated into one another. Add ice if desired, and garnish with a maraschino cherry.
*A single large piece of ice is recommended for serving.

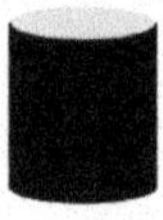

41.

RUSTY NAIL

1.5 oz. scotch
¾ oz. Drambuie
Garnish with a lemon twist

Add scotch and Drambuie to a mixing glass with cubed ice, and stir for 30 seconds to reach optimal temperature. Strain into an Old Fashioned glass, and twist the lemon over the finished drink, also rubbing the peel around the rim of the glass to expose citrus oil, then garnish with it.

*I like to use a scotch with a high peat flavor for this drink as it creates a nice profile with the herbaceous honey flavor of the Drambuie. High peat will be from the Islay (pronounced 'eye-luh) region of Scotland, and lower peat content the more likely the 'lower land' the scotch is from. In fact, Lowland scotch is sometimes called a "lowland lady" for its mellow more floral flavors. Highland scotch is not typically very peaty either, so don't let the name fool you!

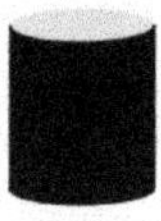

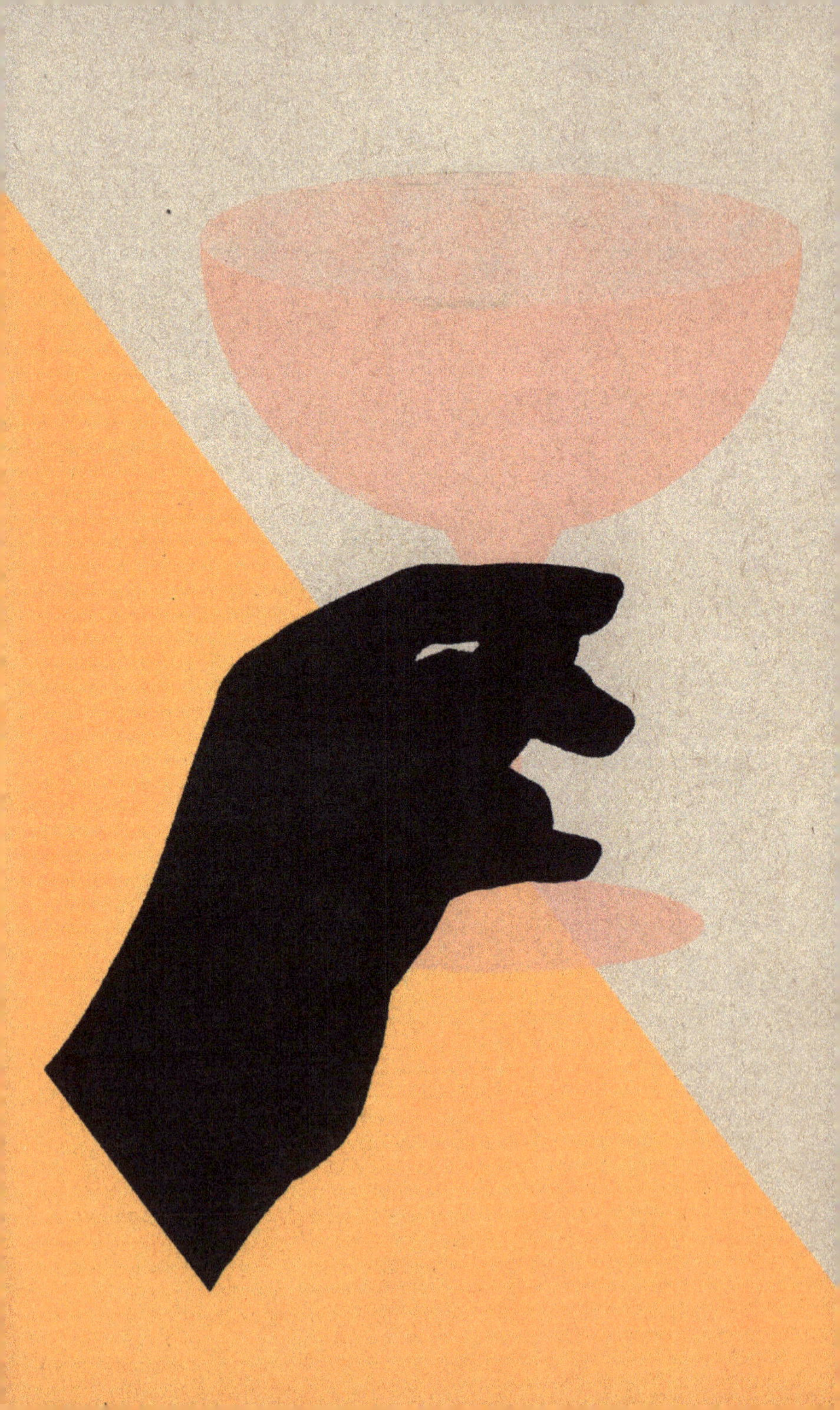

SIDECAR

This popular beverage was invented in the First World War in Paris, said to have been created by one Harry MacElhone, owner of Harry's New York Bar.

2 oz. cognac
¾ oz. lemon juice
¾ oz. orange liqueur (like Cointreau or Grand Marnier)
Granulated sugar
Orange twist for garnish

Add all liquid ingredients to a cocktail shaker with ice and shake until well chilled. Prepare a coupe glass by dipping the rim in water or citrus juice followed by granulated sugar to coat. Strain sidecar into glass; garnish with orange twist and serve.

SCREWDRIVER

*The proportion of vodka to orange juice is totally up to you, but I find that the 1:2 ratio takes the edge off the vodka and keeps the orange juice from being overly sweet.

2 oz. vodka
4 oz. orange Juice

Add all ingredients to a mixing glass over ice, and stir. Strain and serve in a highball glass.

WHISKEY SOUR

*For a less strong bourbon flavor, add an extra ¼ oz. of simple syrup - this mellows out the flavor.

2 oz. bourbon
¾ oz. lemon juice
¾ oz. simple syrup (pp.90)
Orange wheel and/or maraschino cherry for garnish

To make the original sour, add all liquid ingredients to a cocktail shaker with ice, and shake for 20 seconds. Strain, garnish, and serve in an Old Fashioned glass over ice.

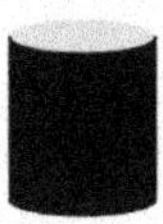

OLD TIMERS

48.

APEROL SPRITZ

One of many spritz beverages, the Aperol spritz dates back to when parts of Italy were still under the control of Austria. This drink is still made there today and consumed by locals and travelers alike. You can find them in almost every bar and restaurant across western Europe.

1.5 oz. classic Aperol liqueur
2 oz. champagne or prosecco
3 to 4 oz. soda water
Orange twist or wedge for garnish

Add Aperol and prosecco to a mixing glass over ice and stir well. Strain into an Old Fashioned, or wine glass, and fill to the top with soda water (between 3-4 ounces). Garnish and serve, and add ice if desired.

BEES KNEES

2 oz. gin

¾ oz. lemon juice

½ oz. honey

Lemon round for garnish

Add all liquid ingredients to a cocktail shaker with crushed ice and shake well until the mix is chilled and the honey is well incorporated. Strain into a coupe glass and garnish with lemon.

*If your honey is thick and difficult to combine when cold, mix 2 parts honey to one part hot water and mix well before adding it to the cocktail shaker, or grab a honey simple syrup to use instead.

*For a lovely summer version, use lavender infused gin, or swap the honey for a botanical simple syrup for added floral notes.

BLUE MONDAY

Curaçao is a type of orange liqueur, so why use it *and* an orange liqueur in the same drink? Other liqueurs, such as Cointreau have a softer, more floral taste, whilst curaçaos (blue or not) have more spice. The combination here is for a marriage of flavors, not just to complicate your day!

1 ½ oz. vodka
½ oz. orange liqueur
½ oz. blue curaçao
Orange twist for garnish

Add all liquid ingredients to a cocktail shaker with ice and shake well until chilled. Strain into a martini glass and . garnish with an orange twist.

51.

CLOVER CLUB

The clover club is a pre-Prohibition drink that originated in Philadelphia. So drink up, it's history!

2 oz. gin
1 oz. raspberry simple syrup
½ oz. lemon juice
1 egg white
3 raspberries for garnish

Add gin, raspberry simple syrup, lemon juice, and egg white to a cocktail shaker, add ice, and shake. Shake until the egg white is thoroughly incorporated; it should be white and frothy and have no solids anywhere in the drink. Strain into a coupe glass and garnish with raspberries.

*Don't have raspberry simple syrup?
Muddle 3 to 4 large raspberries and add plain simple syrup (recipe page 90) to the 1 oz. mark. Mix well and use in the place of premixed syrup. Make sure you strain well in this case, to avoid seeds in the drink.

52.

CORPSE REVIVER

Variations of this cocktail started popping up in the mid 1800's in London bars and pamphlets, and originated as hangover cures or pick-me-ups. I can't say I recommend it to combat overindulgence in alcohol, but it is a tasty addition to a cocktail evening that strays off the beaten path.

Absinthe, to rinse glass
¾ oz. gin
¾ oz. orange liqueur
¾ oz. Lillet Blanc
¾ oz. lemon juice

Rinse the inside of the serving glass (martini or coupe) carefully with absinthe; discard the runoff and set aside. Add all other liquid ingredients into a cocktail shaker, add ice, and shake vigorously until chilled, about 20 seconds. Strain into the absinthe rinsed glass and serve.

53.

GRASSHOPPER

*This New Orleans cocktail is meant as an after dinner beverage, and is minty and fresh for days via the créme de menthe. If entertaining, consider crushing chocolate cookies and either rimming the glass, or adding them directly into the drink for an even sweeter twist, and offer it as your dessert course.

1 oz. half and half (or single cream)
1 oz. créme de menthe
1 oz. white créme de cacao
Mint leaves for garnish

Add all liquid ingredients to a cocktail shaker with ice and shake until chilled and of milkshake consistency. Strain into martini glass and garnish with mint leaves.

KIR ROYALE

1 oz. crème de cassis
4 oz. champagne or prosecco
Blackberry for garnish

Add crème de cassis to a champagne flute and pour over champagne. Garnish with a blackberry. Allow the drinker to stir the ingredients together to create an ombré effect for presentation.

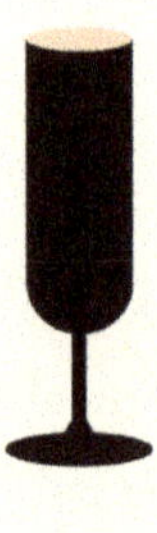

PINK SQUIRREL

Crème de almond is a wonderful liqueur containing exactly what it says, almond. However, it is predated in use by the infamous crème de noyaux, a red tinted, almond-flavored liqueur which is actually made from apricot or other fruit pits. The reason I put both as an option is because crème de noyaux is increasingly difficult to find, and it is being made less and less. The pits from which it is made, and derives its almond flavor contain trace amounts of cyanide (that's actually why it tastes like almond). Though this is in small amounts and is usually completely harmless, the health concerns have limited its availability on the market. Crème de almond still makes a wonderful Pink Squirrel, but you will have to add the coloring in separately or drink it white, as the pink hue of the drink originates from the noyaux.

¾ oz. crème de almond (or crème de noyaux)
¾ oz. white crème de cacao
1½ oz. heavy cream
Maraschino cherry for garnish

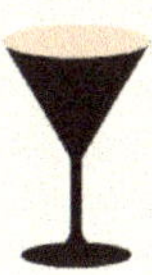

To make this 1950's boozy milkshake, add the liquid ingredients to a cocktail shaker with plenty of ice and shake vigorously until well chilled, and a frothy milkshake consistency. Strain into a coupe glass, and garnish with a maraschino cherry.

LADIES AND GENTLEMEN

BLOODY MARY

*This cocktail is best when served right away, but to prepare it in advance for entertaining I will blend everything but the ice together until right before serving to keep it the right temperature and consistency.

Ingredients: (makes 4 to 6 servings)
32 oz. (4 cups) tomato juice
8 oz. vodka
2 oz. lime juice
2 cloves of garlic, peeled but whole
½ teaspoon celery salt
½ teaspoon pepper
1 teaspoon hot sauce of your choice
1 teaspoon Worcestershire sauce
1 dash of paprika
1 dash of chili powder
1 pinch of sea salt
1-1 1/2 cups of crushed ice

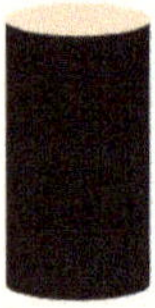

Add all ingredients (minus any garnishes) to a blender with the ice and blend until thick and smooth. Serve in highball glasses, and garnish according to personal tastes.

Popular garnishes include: celery, cilantro, bacon, cheese cubes, peppers, lemons and limes, and pickles.

HUGO

*Elderflowers, in one form or another, can be found all over Europe, especially in the summer. They may be harder to track down stateside, but a quick internet search should help you locate some. I recommend the Swedish brand Darbo.

3 to 4 mint leaves, plus more to garnish
½ oz. lime juice
¾ oz. elderflower syrup
4 oz. prosecco
4 oz. Lillet Blanc

In a mixing glass, muddle the mint in lime juice and elderflower syrup until well infused. Add prosecco and Lillet and stir until well combined into a white wine glass, neat or on the rocks. Garnish with mint leaves.

60.

MADAME CAROLYN

This specific iteration of the cocktail is a family invention which came out of a surplus amount of Makers Mark Whiskey, and limited other cocktail supplies. It is uncomplicated, simple to make, and delicious.

1 oz. bourbon (Maker's Mark Whisky recommended)
3 oz. ginger ale or ginger beer
Juice from one lime wedge and an additional lime wedge to garnish

Add crushed or pebbled ice to lowball glass and add bourbon, ginger ale, and lime juice. Stir well and garnish with additional lime wedge.

61.

ROB ROY

*This one is a sipper for sure. I personally like to garnish with the maraschino cherry as it cuts some of the bitterness of the drink.

¾ oz. sweet vermouth
1 ½ oz. scotch (low peat)
1 dash Angostura aromatic bitters
Maraschino cherry and/or lemon twist for garnish

Add vermouth, scotch, and bitters in a mixing glass with ice and stir. Strain into a martini glass, and garnish with the fruit of your choice. Add fresh ice, if desired.

THE HEMINGWAY

2 oz. white rum
¾ oz. grapefruit juice
¾ oz. dark rum
½ oz. lime juice
¼ oz. maraschino liqueur
¼ oz. simple syrup (pp.90)
Lime wedge for garnish

Add all liquid ingredients to a cocktail shaker with ice and shake for at least 20 seconds, until chilled through. Strain into a martini glass and garnish with a lime wedge.

63.

THE LADY IN VIOLET

3 oz. cranberry juice
1 oz. créme de violette
½ oz. lemon juice
3 oz. prosecco
Fresh berries (blackberries and raspberries) for garnish

Add cranberry juice, créme de violette, and lemon juice to a cocktail shaker with ice and shake well. Strain into a coupe glass, straight, and pour over prosecco. Garnish with fresh berries.

TOM COLLINS

2 oz. dry gin
1 oz. lemon juice
½ oz. simple syrup (pp.90)
4 oz. club soda
Lemon slice and a maraschino cherry for garnish

Add gin, lemon juice, and simple syrup to a cocktail shaker with ice, and shake until chilled. Strain into a collins glass, top with club soda, and garnish with lemon slice and a maraschino cherry.

*if the name sounds vaguely familiar, a 'Vodka Collins' is the same drink, made with vodka instead of gin.

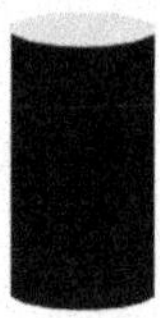

65.

VESPER

3 oz. dry gin
1 oz. vodka
1 oz. Lillet Blanc
Lemon twist for garnish

A classic from 007. To make it Bond's way, add all liquid ingredients to a cocktail shaker with ice, and shake until freezing cold. If you prefer a less diluted, all-spirit cocktail, stir instead of shake the ingredients together. Strain into a martini glass, and serve with a lemon twist.

*Rub your martini glass rim with lemon peel, and twist to express over the glass for extra citrus flavor.

FAR AWAY LANDS

68.

BELLINI

2 oz. peach puree or nectar
4 oz. prosecco
½ oz. simple syrup (pp. 90)
Peach wedge to garnish

Add peach puree and simple syrup to a champagne flute, and pour prosecco over the top. Garnish with peach wedge, and allow the drinker to stir contents.

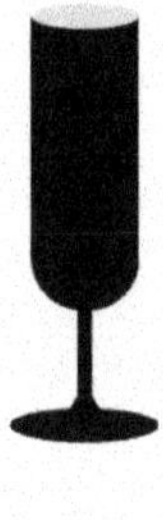

BLUE HAWAIIAN

This 1957 vacation-in-a-glass screams American mid-century aesthetics and tropical vibes. All that's missing is some rock-and-roll and a big ol' pair of shades to complete the scene.

1 oz. blue curaçao liqueur
1 oz. spiced rum
2 ½ oz. pineapple juice
1 ½ oz. coconut cream, unsweetened
Slice of pineapple and a maraschino cherry for garnish

Add all liquid ingredients to a blender with a handful of ice and blend on high until you get a slushy consistency. Serve in a hurricane glass and garnish with tropical fruits.

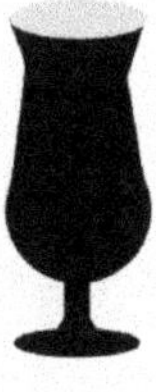

CAPE COD

1 oz. vodka
4 oz. cranberry juice (no sugar added)
Lime wedge for garnish

Combine vodka and cranberry juice in a mixing glass with ice and stir well. Strain into a highball glass and garnish with a lime wedge or wheel to serve.

*For added sweetness, add ½ oz. of lime juice, but if you prefer the sharpness of the cranberry, forgo it.

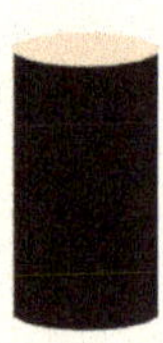

DAIQUIRI

This Caribbean concoction was consumed long before its American popularization in 1909 via Navy soldiers. This is due to the abundance and availability of sugarcane and rum amongst local communities and towns in and around the West Indies.

1 ½ oz. white rum
½ oz. simple syrup (pp. 90)
1 oz. lime juice

Add all ingredients to a cocktail shaker with ice and shake until well chilled. Strain into a martini glass and serve straight.

FUZZY NAVEL

3 oz. peach schnapps
3 oz. orange juice

To make it a Hairy Navel:
1 1/2 oz. peach schnapps
1 1/2 oz. vodka
3 oz. orange juice

Combine peach schnapps and orange juice in a cocktail shaker with ice and shake well. (If making a Hairy Navel, add vodka with other ingredients.) Strain into a highball glass, with fresh ice, if desired.

LONG ISLAND ICED TEA

¾ oz. vodka
¾ oz. white rum
¾ oz. tequila
¾ oz. gin
¾ oz. orange liqueur
¾ oz. simple syrup (pp.90)
¾ oz. lemon juice
2 oz. cola, more to taste
Lemon slice for garnish

Add all liquid ingredients to a mixing glass class with ice and stir well to incorporate. Add more cola to the top to taste. Serve in a highball glass garnished with lemon; sip through a straw.

MAI TAI

1 ½ oz. white rum

½ oz. orange liqueur

½ oz. orgeat syrup

¾ oz. dark rum

½ oz. lime juice

Pineapple wedge, lime round, and/or mint for garnish

Add all liquid ingredients to a shaker with ice and shake until thoroughly chilled. Strain into a highball glass over rocks and garnish with pineapple, lime, and mint. This is best served with a tiny umbrella for a tropical feel, trust me.

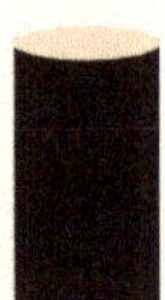

MOSCOW MULE

2 oz. vodka
½ oz. lime juice
6 oz. ginger beer
A lime wedge and mint sprig to garnish

Shake together vodka and lime juice with ice and strain into your cocktail glass (such as a copper Moscow Mule mug or Old Fashioned glass) over fresh crushed ice. Add ginger beer atop, and garnish with lime and mint sprig.

*For a botanical kick, shake the vodka and lime juice with an extra sprig of mint - it will give an added element of freshness!

PAINKILLER

2 oz. spiced dark rum
4 oz. pineapple juice
1 1/2 oz. créme of coconut
1 oz. orange juice
Ground nutmeg for garnish
Pineapple, orange, and lime slices for garnish

Add all liquid ingredients to a cocktail shaker and add ice. Shake for at least 20 seconds, and strain into a glass (extra points if it's fun and tropical) over ice. Add fruit garnishes and grate fresh, or sprinkle ground nutmeg over the top.

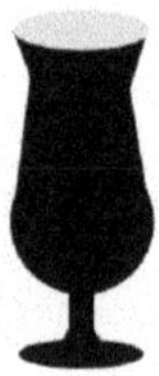

PORN STAR MARTINI

Somewhere around the 4th Arrondissement on a hot summer's day is where I first came across this drink; and maybe it was the magic of Paris or the need to escape the heat that ingrained it in my mind as a welcome refreshment, but it remains a favorite of mine to this day. It was pink, shimmery, and sweet - like a physical embodiment of the city's femininity itself, and I couldn't resist going home and recreating it to reminisce time and time again.

1 1/2 oz. vodka
2 oz. Passoã or other passion fruit liqueur
½ oz. vanilla infused simple syrup (pp.90)
½ oz. lemon juice
1 fresh passion fruit
3 ½ oz. prosecco

Add vodka, Passoã, simple syrup, and lemon juice to a cocktail shaker with ice. Cut a passion fruit in half, scoop out half of the contents and add to the shaker. Shake until chilled, and strain into a coupe glass or martini glass. Add prosecco over top, and float the other half of the passion fruit to garnish.

COLD WEATHER COMPANY

BLACK/WHITE/SPICE RUSSIAN

*Though pumpkin spice gets a bad reputation for being "basic," these fall spice add-ins turn this drink into an extraordinary concoction. Stir or shake them into your Russian of choice and cozy up to this delicious fall drink.

Black Russian
2 oz. vodka
1 oz. Kahlúa

White Russian
2 oz. vodka
1 oz. Kahlúa
½ oz. of heavy cream.

Spice Russian
2 oz. vodka
1 oz. Kahlúa
½ oz. of heavy cream.
2 dashes of cinnamon
2 dashes of nutmeg
1 dash of ginger

BLACK/WHITE/SPICE RUSSIAN

Add vodka and Kahlúa to an Old Fashioned glass over ice, and stir.

If making a White Russian, there are two things you can do:

1. Pour the cream atop and let it swirl in naturally, then stir. This is the extremely photogenic version.
2. Shake all ingredients in a cocktail shaker with ice and strain over fresh ice for a boozy milkshake effect.

If making the spiced version do all previous steps, and add spices and stir before serving. If you are doing a shaken White Russian I recommend shaking the spices in with the heavy cream.

EGGNOG

Eggnog can be drunk hot or cold - I think this recipe is great either way but is especially festive hot. If you are drinking it cold: chill completely (anywhere from 3 hours to overnight) and serve.

(serves 4-6)
6 egg yolks
½ cup granulated sugar
⅛ cup light brown sugar
16 oz. (2 cups) milk (2% to whole in fat content)
8 oz. (1 cup) heavy whipping cream, more for garnish
A pinch of salt
1 teaspoon ground nutmeg, more for garnish
1 teaspoon ground cinnamon, more for garnish
1 vanilla bean pod
6 to 8 oz. spiced rum

Add egg yolks and sugars to a medium bowl and whisk until well combined; set aside.

In a pot over medium heat, mix cream, milk, salt, nutmeg, and cinnamon, whisking together to incorporate. Slice the vanilla bean lengthwise and scrape the seeds into the cream mixture, then drop the whole bean pod in the pot to steep while it heats.

EGGNOG

When your dairy mixture has warmed through, but not boiled, temper the eggs in slowly while you whisk consistently (this avoids cooking the egg and causing clumps later on). Stir for at least 30 seconds after combining to ensure a smooth incorporation. Add rum to mixture in desired amount. The darker the rum you use, the stronger the alcohol flavor will be. I like to use a medium spiced rum as it brings out the other spices and keeps the drink smooth in flavor. Whisk over heat for 30 seconds, then remove from heat.

Take additional heavy cream and whip until light and fluffy. Garnish individual servings with whipped cream and a dusting of cinnamon and nutmeg.

*If your Eggnog seems a little thin after all ingredients are added, don't worry just yet. Even with 2% milk, when cooled the mixture thickens on its own. However if you do need to thicken further, keep over heat until you see a slight consistency change, then remove to avoid total solidification. This might be necessary if using a dairy alternative milk.

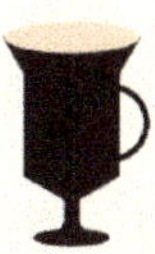

HOT TODDY

While this drink is delicious and not purely medicinal, it has a history of being an aid to the common cold, and other congestive ailments. As my Grandfather would say, "It never hurts to sanitize the inside too!" And the cleansing lemon, soothing honey, and medicinal cinnamon certainly won't hinder a speedy recovery!

8 oz. water
2 oz. whiskey
½ oz. honey
½ oz. lemon juice
1 cinnamon stick (or a few dashes ground cinnamon)
Lemon slice and additional cinnamon stick for garnish

In a pot over medium heat, add all liquid ingredients and bring to a low simmer for 1 to 2 minutes; add the cinnamon to infuse its flavor into the mixture. Pour into a heat resistant glass, preferably one with a handle to protect your hands, and garnish with lemon slice and additional cinnamon stick.

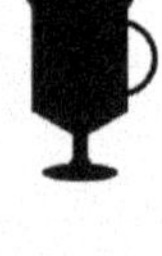

IRISH COFFEE

2 oz. Irish whiskey
6 oz. freshly brewed dark coffee
Freshly whipped cream and cinnamon for garnish

Add Irish whiskey to your Irish Coffee mug (or other cocktail glass) and pour the hot coffee over the top. Mix well with a spoon or other stirring implement, and garnish with whipped cream and cinnamon.

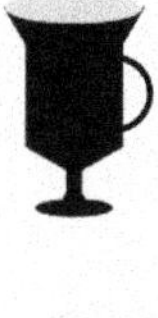

JACK THE RIPPER

Jack the Ripper is like a crisp caramel apple on a perfect sunny fall day—it has bite, sweetness, and a little bit of spice. It makes a fantastic cocktail for social gatherings or a special treat for one!

3 oz. Irish whiskey
2 oz. butterscotch schnapps
1 dash of cinnamon
Caramel sauce (to rim the glass)

In a cocktail shaker, combine whiskey, schnapps, and cinnamon with ice. Shake for at least 20 seconds. Rim a cocktail class with caramel sauce, and strain the shakers contents into it. Add ice if desired.

*A single large piece of ice is recommended for serving

PIMM'S PUNCH

*This recipe doubles and triples well, so multiply as you see fit for entertainment purposes. A punchbowl of this has never led me astray when hosting a holiday get-together.

(serves 2-4)
6 oz. cranberry juice
2 oz. Pimm's No. 1
½ oz. lemon juice
4 oz. prosecco
4 oz. ginger ale
Fresh cranberries, orange slices, and mint

In a large bowl or pitcher, combine cranberry juice, Pimm's, and lemon juice, then top with the carbonated items (prosecco and ginger ale). Stir well, and add ice if desired. Garnish with cranberries, orange slices, and mint to personal tastes while still in the bowl or pitcher. Serve in a coupe.

FURTHER RECIPES

SIMPLE SYRUP

*Why simple syrup instead of just sugar? Well, we've all had a cocktail or glass of iced tea with sugar that wouldn't dissolve in the bottom because it was too cool. Simple syrup eliminates that potential problem, as it is already in liquid form and incorporates with far more ease. No more "bevvies" with less sweetener than you bargained for!

If making an infused version, add your fruit or herb of choice just after the sugar dissolves, and let it "steep" for the same amount of time as you would the pure sugar and water, then strain any solids out before storing. Some delicious infusions are: vanilla beans, ginger, rose, and mint.

1 cup granulated sugar
1 cup water

Combine sugar and water in a medium saucepan and bring to a boil, stirring to incorporate and dissolve the sugar without letting it burn on the bottom. When the mixture boils, reduce to a medium heat, and simmer until the mixture thickens just slightly. Remove from heat and allow to cool to room temperature before using. Keep in the refrigerator, it's good until it starts to crystallize at a maximum of three weeks.

CANDIED CITRUS FRUIT

*While fresh citrus rounds are already delish, a nice way to prepare them for fall drinks, or add an extra element of sweetness, is to candy them. When they're finished, they should be slightly stiffer than a fresh lemon round or slice, which makes them great for decorative purposes in cocktails and a multitude of desserts. They're super tasty and can be eaten just like candy, rind and all.

2-3 citrus fruits of choice - sliced thinly in rounds.
½ cup sugar

Preheat the oven to 250°F (120°C), and line a baking sheet with aluminum foil. Toss citrus rounds in sugar to coat and place in a single layer on the lined baking sheet. Bake for 1 hour and 15 minutes, checking for burning and rotating the pan every 15 minutes. Remove from the oven and allow them to cool on the baking sheet before using. To store, place in an airtight container for about two weeks. This recipe dries the fruit so it does not need to be refrigerated.

CITRUS SUGAR

*This recipe works for salt as well to add a zesty addition to your savory cocktail rims. Just swap the sugar out for a salt!

Zest of citrus fruit of choice
(1 if large, such as an orange, 2 if small, like limes)
2 cups granulated sugar

Zest your citrus fruit, taking care to only add the colored portions and not the bitter white rind (called the pith). Add to a bowl with the sugar and thoroughly combine.
Line a baking tray with parchment paper; spread the sugar mixture in an even layer, and leave out to dry for 24 hours, gently stirring or shaking occasionally to avoid clumps forming. Use the baking tray liner to funnel the citrus sugar into an airtight storage container and store in a cool dry place.

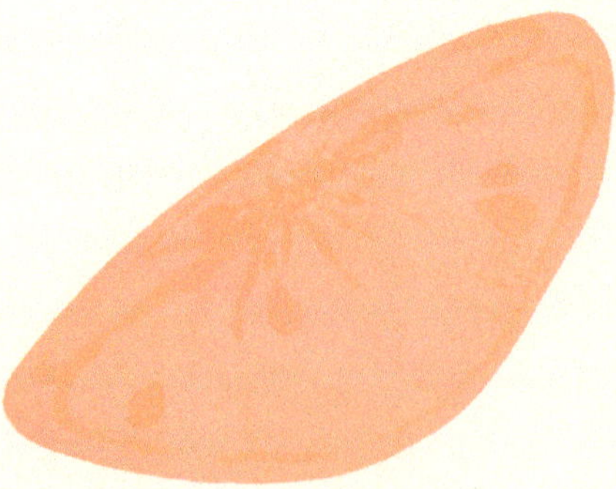

What's a nice kid like me doing in a place like this?

Drinking.

GLOSSARY OF TERMS

ABV - The initialism for "alcohol by volume," ABV is a measurement system of the percentage of alcohol contained in a bottle of spirit or liquor. It deals with how much ethanol (measured in milliliters) is contained within 100 milliliters of solution. While some other measurement systems are utilized in various places in the world, the ABV method is used worldwide.

Bitters - An alcoholic concoction flavored with botanicals such as herbs, spices, and flowers making a concentrate with a bitter or bittersweet flavor profile. Originally used as medicines to aid in various conditions such as digestion, they are now primarily used as cocktail flavorings.

Dash - Officially between 8 and 10 drops. This would be between 2 or 3 longish turns of the bottle over whatever you are adding them to.

Liqueur and Liquor - Liquor refers to any alcoholic drink, especially those brewed or distilled. These are commonly drunk alone as well as mixed.
Liqueur on the other hand is any sweet alcoholic drink, composed of alcohol and the sugars, fruits, and other elements steeped in the alcohol.

GLOSSARY OF TERMS

Liqueurs are rarely drunk alone, and are often added to cocktails and sometimes cooking and baking.

Muddle - To mix and crush, much like the movements used with a mortar and pestle. This is usually done to combine ingredients and to infuse herb and or fruit flavors into other ingredients. There is a special tool for this called a muddler, but the task can also be achieved with a spoon or other kitchen utensil.

Neat - To serve a drink "neat" means serving the concoction without ice.

Overproof - Containing more alcohol percentage per volume than the standard distilled spirit—this must be more than 50 percent ABV.

Proof - The measurement of proof is simply double the ABV. Any alcohol with 100 proof or higher is called a "proof spirit" sometimes "Bottled in Bond." Aside from the importance of measuring the content of alcohol in a spirit, the system was developed because in some parts of the world (namely England), a higher tax could be placed on alcohols that contained a higher content of ethanol.

GLOSSARY OF TERMS

Rocks - Ice. "On the Rocks" means to serve a drink with ice.

Schnapps - Similar to a liqueur, schnapps are sweet fruit and herb additive alcohols that are usually steeped and fermented in grain-based alcohols.

Smacking - Slapping or hitting something *gently* against the back of your hand, wrist, or between the palms to release flavors and essences. Do this with all herbs before garnishing or adding them into shakers and mixing glasses.

Twist - A twist, generally of citrus, is a long segment of peel with zest used to garnish a drink. They are made by peeling a long thin segment directly off of the fruit, and twisting it over the drink to expose it. Rubbing the fruit twist along the rim of the glass is also highly recommended in order to fully experience the flavor. The longer the piece, the more naturally it will curl on its own, like it naturally would hugging the fruit. However, if you only peel short pieces, they can be hand rolled and run through with a toothpick or cocktail pick to maintain their shape, rested along the edge of the glass. Trimming the edges is recommended for a clean line; and the more you practice, the more intricate the design of your twists can get.

INDEX

INDEX

INDEX

ABOUT THE AUTHOR

Natalie E. Brown is an international artist and scholar devoted to vintage, nostalgic, and emotionally inquisitive imagery. She works in both illustration and digital photography, as well as in a gallerist capacity. Her work is generally recognized for a dark theatricality and energetic drama, as well as her use of traditional methods for the creation of contemporary art. *Butcher, Baker, Cocktail Maker: A Guide to Making and Shaking* is her second publication, and first cocktail making or cookery book.

She is assisted in all endeavors both artistic and academic by a menagerie of small dogs and cats, and splits her time between Maine, and Germany.

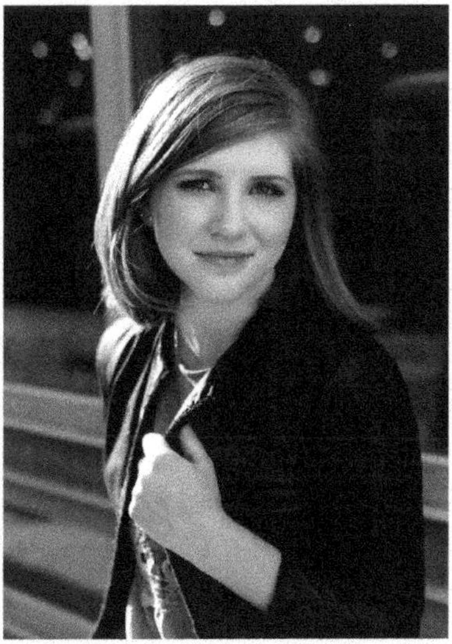

ABOUT THIS BOOK

Born out of necessity, other times luxury and extravagance, cocktails have existed for centuries, serving as mankind's splendid distraction from the mundane, and often a symbol of celebration.

Brown follows old favorites, and new discoveries in the world of craft cocktails, celebrating what and when you mix (in 50 plus recipes) no matter how random or small the occasion, delving into the circumstances in which they came about in history and folklore, often with cheeky surprises.

Butcher, Baker, Cocktail Maker: A Guide to Making and Shaking is for anyone with an interest in quality cocktails, emphasizing accessibility regardless of previous knowledge and focusing on the enjoyment of a good drink for sommeliers and novices alike.

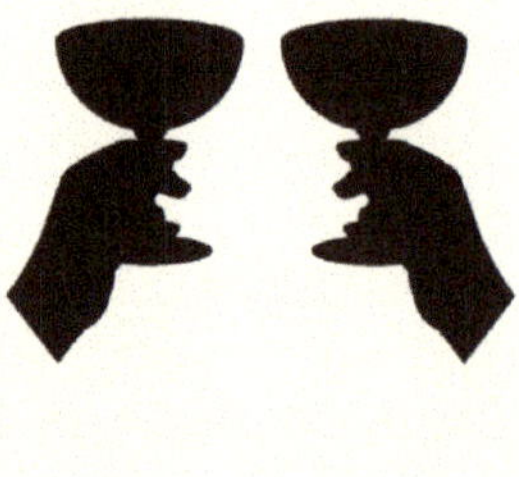

www.ingramcontent.com/pod-product-compliance
Ingram Content Group UK Ltd.
Pitfield, Milton Keynes, MK11 3LW, UK
UKHW060117010826
14089UKWH00004B/30

9 780578 918402